Edmund Vance Cooke

A Patch Of Pansies

Edmund Vance Cooke

A Patch Of Pansies

ISBN/EAN: 9783744651776

Printed in Europe, USA, Canada, Australia, Japan

Cover: Foto ©ninafisch / pixelio.de

More available books at **www.hansebooks.com**

A PATCH OF PANSIES

BY

J. EDMUND V. COOKE

G. P. PUTNAM'S SONS
NEW YORK　　　　　　　LONDON
27 West Twenty-third Street　　24 Bedford Street, Strand
The Knickerbocker Press
1894

COPYRIGHT, 1894
BY
J. EDMUND V. COOKE

Entered at **Stationers' Hall, London**
By G. P. Putnam's Sons

Electrotyped, Printed and Bound by
The Knickerbocker Press, New York
G. P. Putnam's Sons

AUTHOR'S NOTE.

It is with sincere pleasure that I acknowledge my obligations to those editors and publishers who have so readily and cheerfully granted me permission to reprint my verses, which have appeared in their publications; and the oft-accompanying expressions of goodwill and kind wishes for this little volume are even more grateful. My explicit thanks are due to Forrest Morgan and the Travelers Insurance Co., Chas. A. Dana and The Sun Publishing Co., the editor of *St. Nicholas* and The Century Co., Keppler and Schwarzmann, publishers of *Puck*, the editor of *Truth* and the Truth Company, the editor and publishers of *The Club*, Dr. T. L. Flood and *The Chautauquan*, the editor of *Life* and Life Publishing Co., C. B. De La Vergne, Jr., and Smith, Gray & Co., the D. Lothrop Co., *The Detroit Free Press*, Susan Hayes Ward and *The Independent*, Chas. W. Handy, Overland Monthly Publishing Co., Arthur B. Tournure and *Vogue* and *Cleveland Town Topics*.

CONTENTS.

	PAGE
Author's Note	iii
The Riddle of the Clock	3
Ambition	5
On the Shore	6
The Tragic Muse	7
Gayety	8
New Year's Eve	9
Grief	10
Unweeping or Unwept	11
The Poet's Song	12
A Triplet of Quatrains	13
Love's Imagery	17
Rondeau—A Mistletoe Spray	19
Perfume	20
Love to Anger	21
Love Song—Unrest	22

CONTENTS.

	PAGE
HUMILITY TO PRIDE	23
THE SONG YOU SANG FOR ME	24
"THE PARTING GUEST"	25
RETROSPECTION	26
I WOULD	28
PHILOPENA	29
CONCEIT	33
TO A BLACK EYE	34
NATURE	35
A COMPOUND FRACTURE	36
THE TEACHER DID	37
RONDEAU—EN PASSANT	38
UNRESPONSIVE	39
THE NAKED TRUTH	40
"THE RULING PASSION"	41
AN AFTER THOUGHT	42
SUB ROSA	43
ETYMOLOGY	44
A "DASHING MAIDEN"	45
MY OWN SWEET HEART	47
THE SADDEST THING	48
REQUIESCAT IN PACE	49

CONTENTS.

	PAGE
"Found Wanting"	50
The Tender-Hearted Man	53
Over the Get-there Road	57
The Ascetic—Up to Date	60
The Other One was Booth	63
A Courtin' Call	66
The Old Man Knows	68
Laugh a Little Bit	70
Leopold	73
The New St. Nicholas	76
A Watchword	81
Consolation	84
"On the Judgmunt Day"	85
"Aufwiederseh'n"	89

PROEM.

Why does he show his pansies planted there?
There are so many, many flowers more rare,
So many wondrous gardens past compare,
What can he hope for, save a passing stare?

Well, when a man has planted them with care,
Has dug and tended, watered all he dare,
Watched every glimpse of green which tinged the bare,
Black earth, known every leaflet there,
Blest every bud with an especial prayer,
Noted each color warm the ambient air,
Seen every blossom's cheek take on its fair,
Soft velvet,—surely we can spare
Some small excuse for him, if he declare
His humble blossoms worthy of a share
Of our regarding.

          Then, too, be aware
The toiler is repaid if he may bear
One touch of brightness to a world of care,
One blossom for a village maiden's hair,
One bit of bloom to glow—and wither—where
A dead child lies, whose peaceful features wear
A smile of wonder at its friends' despair.

Oft when he strove for deeper, rarer color,
The casual comment only called it duller.

To FORREST MORGAN, OF HARTFORD, CONN.,
EDITOR, LITTERATEUR, CRITIC, FRIEND, TO WHOSE ABLE WORDS
AND KIND ACTS I HAVE SO OFTEN BEEN INDEBTED,
I INSCRIBE THESE MOST THOUGHTFUL
OF MY VERSES.

I

THE RIDDLE OF THE CLOCK.

A LONELY poet all devoid of wings
(Which men say *Genius* has) to fly,
Was training him some thoughts (those stubborn things)
To aid him to his goal. The hours flew by,
And as they passed, his patient time-piece broke
Upon his thought. Thereon the poet spoke:

> "Curses on thee, slave of Time!
> With thy dull, insistent chime;
> With thy hands which point the way
> Where the night gropes toward the day;
> With thy calm, unrestful face
> Ever staring into space:
> How thy constancy doth mock
> All *my* restless strife, O clock!
>
> "Ha! Thou art a very Sphinx
> Staring, placid, and methinks
> That thy riddle, still unread,
> Is *that* which thou just hast said.

"Whose those dozen monotones!
Yesternight's last dying moans?
Or the Pallas-shouts, thus freeing,
As the new day leaps to being?
Symbols of the death and birth,
Both in one, of things of Earth?
Both in one?   Then in that blending
Can *beginning* be, *or ending?*

"Or by that repeated strain
Of monotonous refrain,
Dost thou aim to tell us how
Time is never aught but *Now?*
That we are as evanescent
As that ever-passing Present?

"'T is thy riddle, not devolving
On a humble bard for solving.
'T is the riddle of the ages
Still disputed by the sages.
Where, O, where the Œdipus
Who will solve it now for us?"

He ceased, and still the old clock's face
With stolid stare looked into space,
And still it guided on its way
The blind Night groping towards the day.

AMBITION.

AMBITION, comrade-mine, I lag, I tire;
    The heights which you would aid me to, arise
   So far away, nor stop for clouds or skies.
The wondrous peak, to which I've dared aspire,
I've only known by echoes from a lyre
    Touched by a Byron; or when my dim eyes
      Through Shakespeare's glass have seen, and, made more wise,
Have feared to look upon my soul's desire.

And yet I do not murmur at the steeps;
   But hard is this unvaried, low extent
Whose weary length before Parnassus creeps.
   Oh, joyfully I'd try the rough ascent:
Though staffless, worn, and tried by fearful leaps,
   I'd toil toward the stars, and be content.

ON THE SHORE.

THE lustful Storm-King seized the sobbing Sea,
  While pander Darkness lent his dreaded pall
  And bugler Wind blew out a battle-call.
The Thunder laughed in gruff and dismal glee;
The Sky cloud-veiled her eyes, fain not to see,
  Nor plea nor protest rose among them all;
  When lo! a circled light pierced through the thrall,
Touching the Sea's breast with its purity.

I lightly mused:—"A Cyclops' lidless eye?
Or jewel discarded by the mourning sky?"
  Then, "Nay, is't not the Sea's soul, calm and clear
—Though all her form racked by the Storm-fiend lie,—
  And smiling at the powers of Force and Fear?"
  O love! so were my soul if thou wert near.

THE TRAGIC MUSE.

WHEN first he wooed Melpomene, he cried,
   "Muse, to my grief lend thou thy sounding phrase
   And men shall yield me amaranthine bays?"
"Doth Grief chase gaudy bubbles?" she replied.
   Abashed he clutched the grave reproof. "I'll hide
   My sorrow through the weary coming days,
   Nor seek to sob it sweetly in my lays—"
"Does Sorrow sorrow less when undescried?"

He stooped his head. At length he saw aright,
   Then said, "Teach me, O wisest Muse, to show
   The glow of humanizing force in woe,
To star the darkness of the sombre night,
And show how paths of pain lead up to light!"
   And then he heard an "Amen" clear and low.

GAYETY.

KNOW'ST thou alluring Gayety and these
    Who tread within her toilsome, tiresome mill,
Doing the penance of her frivolous will?
Not Tantalus nor Sisyphus seeks ease
More vainly than this band of devotees,
    Who climb a constantly receding hill,
    Who drink a draught which cloys, but does not fill,
Who surfeit self, but may not self appease.

A glance at Gayety seems all delight,
For every Circe is at first most kind,
But envy not the ones who have enshrined
    The siren as a goddess. Folly's rite
    Instills a lightness not of heart, but mind,
And constant sweets make ill the appetite.

NEW YEAR'S EVE.

THE prophet Youth sings triumphs to be won ;
    Age is content because he can remember ;
The gallant, good Old Year's great deeds are done ;
    He leans upon his Minister, December.

His body-guard of days has fought the fight ;
    Grim Death completes the triumph of Disaster ;
Earth weeps her lord and sympathizing Night
    Drapes black about her ; so farewell, old Master.

But now, the moon unveils her clouded face ;
    Earth feels her kiss in pure maternal pleasure ;
And January with a rough, rude grace,
    Offers the infant Year a host of treasure.

Good morning, bright New Year, and here's a toast
    To all the good you find us worth the giving ;
Good night, Old Year; we mourn your death the most
    By giving royal welcome to the living.

GRIEF.

GRIEF is not evil, though its cause
    Seems ill to our believing,
For who, though he could form the laws
Which rule us all, but what would pause
    Before he banished grieving?

Couldst thou be saved from thy distress,
    Be saved from earnest sorrow,
Be sure thy nature then were less
And might not hold the happiness
    Reserved for some to-morrow.

The cup which makes thy lips afraid
    May prove a kind nepenthe;
The gloom may be refreshing shade
To rest thee, like a wooded glade,
    When summer suns have spent thee.

Man did not rise above the beast
    Till he could grieve in season,
Nor shall his woe and pain have ceased,
Till north nor south nor west nor east
    Shall give grief cause or reason.

UNWEEPING OR UNWEPT.

"UNWEPT, unhonored, and unsung"
　　Were not the worst of Fortune's bringing;
Dread, rather, thine own eyes and tongue
　　Unweeping and unsinging.
Unweeping for thy brother, bound
　　But struggling in the sombre Night,
Unsinging from thy vantage-ground
　　The happy tidings of the Light.

Weep and be sure thou shalt be wept.
　　Sing gladly, and the joy-sounds ringing
May wake some soul, which long hath slept,
　　To echo back thy singing.
Let fall thy tears ! Let rise thy strain !
　　So canst thou never be among
Those heritors of man's disdain,
　　Th' "unwept, unhonored, and unsung."

THE POET'S SONG.

THE poet's tuneful voice brought forth a song,
    A song whose words were solace, and whose breath,
Might resurrect dead hope. The troubled throng
    Who tread life's shortening highway down to death,
        Heard with their hearts, and in their varied ways
        They viewed life under brighter, lighter rays;
    Whereat they cried aloud the singer's praise.

They did not know he made his perfect song
    To cheer *himself*, and not the world about,
Nor that he pitched it true and clear and strong
    To drown the voices of unfaith and doubt.
        Oh, it is well that none may singly own
        A touch of beauty, thought, nor tint, nor tone:
    Though born of him, it is not his alone.

A TRIPLET OF QUATRAINS.

POETRY.

To deftly do what many dimly think ;
    To fund a feeling for the world to borrow ;
To turn a tear to printer's ink ;
    To make a sonnet of a sorrow.

EGO-THEISM.

This trouble seems to be
    Chief in theology :
Each thinks the hymn should be,—
    Nearer, *my* God, to Thee.

THE MYSTERY OF EVIL.

The rake upon a wanton wastes the wiles
    Which dazzle innocence.
The nettle guards itself ; the lily smiles
    Unheedful of defence.

*What, though the flowers be humble; should he care,
If lovely woman deem them fit to wear?*

TO THAT WOMAN OF WOMEN,
MY MOTHER,
I DEDICATE THESE LOVE-VERSES,
AND THROUGH HER I GREET MY MANY OTHER WOMEN-FRIENDS,
FAR AND NEAR, OLD AND YOUNG.

LOVE'S IMAGERY.

I.

LOVE is a bubbling, sparkling brook,
    Springing up from any nook,
Sunning itself as it lolls along,
Singing a snatch of happy song,
Thinking the world but a gentle hill
To speed the course of a careless rill.

II.

Love is a river, broadening, deepening,
With eddying spots and borders steepening;
And who can stay or guide its course
As on it rolls with gathering force?
And who can say to where 't is tending,
Whether to gliding, peaceful ending,
Or whither the rapids beat the rocks
In constant, endless, sudden shocks,
Till wearied and weak by hopeless fight,
They madly leap Niagara's height?

III.

Love is an ocean, wide as life,
But rippled and waved by smallest strife.
Every cloud that appears in air
Shadows the surface here or there.
Shifting winds and storms of doubt
Trouble and surge and sweep about,
And the tide of passion's awful force
Comes flooding along its heedless course.
But often the sky is blue, and oft
The sun is warm and the breeze is soft,
And whatever the strife that stirs its breast,
Deep, deep down is a perfect rest.

RONDEAU—A MISTLETOE SPRAY.

A MISTLETOE spray—so parched, so dry,
    But the rarest blossom fails to vie,
As I hold it these brief feet in air,
And see !—again she is standing there,
As pure and bright as the summer sky.
Nay, summer similes scarce apply.
'T is a long-sped Christmas calls this sigh,
And only the fair yule-time may wear
    A mistletoe spray.

Sweet, on that day-of-the-days, when I
    Dreamed the boy-god sped his shafts awry,
        This it was told me to do and dare ;
        You under this in your sun-spun hair ;
This—so I treasure it till I die—
    A mistletoe spray !

PERFUME.

A TINY, wandering sylphid brushed my lips,
    As sped she from a field flower to the sky.
  In that brief instant, as she passed me by,
A flutter of the diaphanic tips
Of ether wings waved dainty, grateful sips
    Of half-forgot perfume to me, and I
    Was fain to close my lids and softly sigh,
And lo! to-day for me was in eclipse.

The ghosts of glimmering stars of that last night;
    A witchery of voice, of glance, of dress,
    An echo of a softly spoken "Yes,"
Lived once again. Then the disturbing light
Of this unblest to-day put forth its blight,
    And all the fragrance turned to bitterness!

LOVE TO ANGER.

DEAR one, 't is less of a task, I surmise,
    For brows to be placid, than frowningly knit;
And surely no voice should discordantly rise
    When music were less of an effort for it.

We are so heedless, love, when we are sure.
    Once, what Cupid's service came ever amiss?
Then Anger dissembled and Love would endure,
    And harshest reproach was a vehement kiss.

Love, let those days come again and remain,
    For kisses can punish as well as reward;
You *could* not give any more chastening pain
    Than caresses of anger, still showing regard.

LOVE SONG—UNREST.

LOVE did not come with a rushing wing
  To storm and seize my breast,
But he came as a nameless little thing
With trifles to do and say and sing;
  Pleasant were they, yet brought unrest,
  Pleasant, yet brought unrest.

Anon, his voice took serious ring
  And then command expressed,
And lo! I found that I could not bring
My heart from its mad, mad worshipping
  At the shrine of a wild unrest,
  The shrine of a wild unrest.

I weep with joy and with sorrow sing;
  O, am I curst or blest?
Troubled am I if to me love cling,
But lost am I if away love wing,
  So kiss me, Love, as I kiss Unrest;
  Kiss me! I kiss Unrest!

HUMILITY TO PRIDE.

OUR arms close comrades? In your stately face
    My gayness mirrored? Your proud voice and
      mine
In pleased companionship? It is a grace
    Diogenes himself would scarce decline.

I had not known this sweet and strange surprise,
    Not known delight's soft fragrance such as this,
Had I the joy to see *love* light your eyes,
    To clasp you close and feel your luscious kiss.

For dainty vines embrace the meanest tree;
    And little Cupid, when he draws his bow,
Is blinder than his slaves, or if he see,
    He cares not if his aim be high or low.

The ardent sun of love shines not for me,
    But mine the clear, ideal stars to view;
And I am proudly pleased that Fate's decree
    Grants me these passionless bright smiles from you.

THE SONG YOU SANG FOR ME.

OH, SWEETER, more sweet than the cultured tone
    Of an opera singer's soaring notes,
Or the birds' glad glee, or the waves' sad moan,
    Or the tuneful tinkle of art-made throats
Was the song you sang for me alone and all the world was June,
Was the song you sang—'t was all our own—and my heart beat rhythmic tune.

The saddening charm of a loved refrain
    Is treasured in memory's wide-spaced vaults;
Forever and aye does the charm remain,
    Though the strain surrenders to Time's assaults,
And memory only recalls for me some wandering, straggling part;
Like a Cupid's sob or a Psyche's sigh it echoes through my heart.

Your lips gave each number a soft caress
    And bade it forever a fond good-bye;
'T would be wondrous then if I prized them less
    And did not dream with a wishful sigh.
O singer, the poet's words were naught and the song without a key,
Till into those words you breathed your thought and gave them a life for me.

"THE PARTING GUEST."

"Maiden, from beyond the Rhine,
   Liebchen, with the lips of wine,
Were these lips to visit thine,
What would those lips say to mine?"
Thus I spoke unto my dear,
Who knows my heart and has no fear,
"Liebchen, with the lips of wine,
What would those lips say to mine?"

Said that maiden in reply,
—She who loves as well as I—
"Gentle sir, thy speech is plain,
But should these lips entertain
Thy bold lips, mine own were fain
Just to say 'Aufwiederseh'n,'
To repeat the old refrain
'We'll meet again; Aufwiederseh'n!'"

So, whene'er those lips meet mine
And I quaff their nectared wine,
When they part, they pout again
And that means "Aufwiederseh'n;"
And we swear by that caress,
We shall never love the less,
For our hearts shall still remain
True to that "Aufwiederseh'n."

RETROSPECTION.

'TWERE better had we never met,
      And yet,
Our meeting I can not regret.
Because the day has passed and night set in,
Why should one wish the day had never been?

Why did we only say "Good-bye?"
      A sigh,
A word, had given doubt the lie.
One ardent smile had been a golden ray
To melt the coolness, which between us lay.

The radiant brightness of a glance,
      Perchance,
Had lightened shaded circumstance.
A single glimmering, regretful tear
Had washed away my dismal, doubting fear.

No token came. We said " Farewell."
                      It fell
Like low-rung, sad-tongued, solemn knell ;
And like a spirit's sigh it haunted me,
And 't was a ghost of woe, which was to be.

O truant thoughts ! why roam so far
                      To mar
The beauties of the things that are?
'T is folly thus, to look, with saddened sigh,
For vanished love-light when the day is by.

I WOULD.

I WOULD write of you, love, in an ode or a sonnet.
  For the theme were a garb to the muse who might don it
(Though flounced as an epic, or cut as a ballad)
To heighten what charm she possesses,
And lighten the faults she confesses
  And brighten her visage, no matter how pallid.

If my pen were that shaft which the boy-god let sink
In my heart and the fluid it touched were the ink,
  I'd praise you in rubrics commanding inspection;
But, dear, every thought is so true
In loving allegiance to you,
  It leaves me to flee in your pleasing direction.

Yea, the Laura of Petrarch might envy the lyric
And Beatrice covet the poem-panegyric;
  And Fame would, perforce, own you Queen of the Graces.
'T were done, were it not for the crimes
Of metre and rhythm and rhymes;
  They shirk, while I work, and they *won't* keep their places.

PHILOPENA.

ROGUISH, *chic, petite* Helena
    Ate with me a philopena.
" Now," she cried, " 't is give and take ;
You must keep your wits awake ;
Not an instant be remiss,
Though I proffer you a kiss."
Ere her voice had ceased expressing,
My lips to her lips were pressing.

Triumph conquered indignation,
And with gleeful exclamation,
" Philopena ! " clamored she,
" For you took a kiss from me."
" Nay, my wise one, nay, not so ;
I did but a kiss bestow.
You accepted it, Helena,
And from me, hence—philopena ! "

" Ah ! " she cried, " if it 's contested,
I 'm becoming interested.

We 'll begin anew to try
Who shall conquer, you or I.
I 'll be ever on my guard;
Every glance from you I 'll ward;
If a muscle to you cater,
Atrophy may seize the traitor."

Then I pleaded: "Lovely maiden,
Take *me* and my heart o'erladen
With the love it brings to you."
White lids veil her eyes of blue,
And her warm heart tints her cheeks,
Till at length she slowly speaks:
"Muscles of the heart, you know,
Are involuntary, so
You have won, for they *will* take you.
What gift, victor, shall I make you?"

"Gift! Oh, I am paid, Helena;
Be *yourself* the philopena.
Had I lost you, ghoulish pain,
Wed with sorrow—wretched twain!—
Would have seized my broken heart
And devoured it, part and part,
As we, O, my sweet Helena,
Ate that blissful philopena."

A parti-colored bunch of brighter hue
May win the grace of merry men like you.

TO BRADLEY H. PHILLIPS, OF BUFFALO, N. Y.

'TIS not alone I love *you* well, dear Bradley,
   Induces me to pen these lines to you,
For these same lines must tell (although so badly)
A hundred friends I love them as I do.
There's Newton, Robert, Harry—very gladly
I'd put the hundred here, (if this were guerdon),
But faith! the names would crowd each other sadly,
So let your senior friendship bear the burden.

CONCEIT.

CONCEIT, the world may hear me! I confess
    That once I loved thee. This much do I own
   Nor say it in a light nor covert tone,
As men oft own a folly. The distress
Of failure thou couldst soothe, or doubly bless
    A slender triumph. Thou, and thou alone,
    Hadst faith in me, when all the world had flown.
Good sooth! but mortals oft are loved for less.

But constant to me as I thought thee, thou
    Hast raised a frenzy that I may not quell,
For lo! thy kiss is on another's brow,
    (Deny it not, Conceit, for I can tell)
    And though, when mine, I loved thee passing well,
Since thou art his, contempt doth gorge me now.

TO A BLACK EYE.

CIMMERIAN optic! how thou hast possessed
    My little world's attent. When thou wert fair
    And like thy fellow, void of vicious air,
None with thy character seemed much impressed.
Now, in thy purple and fine linen dressed
    E'en modest maidens, passing, at thee stare,
    Although they never met thee otherwhere.
In former days, unstained, wert thou so blest?

Ah, Virtue's even course runs on for aye,
    And no one marks it. Good is reckoned *nil*.
So runs the world. Said any yesterday
    "Thy dexter optic! lo, how free from ill!"
Yet now, meseems, the very asses bray
    And o'er thy blackened woe hee-haw their fill.

NATURE.

I STOOD within the city park, and sad
  Was I to see that sordid man had left
So little love for Nature ; was so reft
Of his innate simplicity by mad
And selfish struggles with the world to add
    Gold unto gold. " He keeps his marts of theft,
    Counting that robber greatest, who most deft,
Nor knows he 's thralled, while freedom here is had.

" How strange are human preference and choice
    Which revel in the town's tumultuous din,
Nor seek this place where mankind may rejoice
    In peace, as erst they did ere towns had been ! "

As thus I mused, there came a sudden voice,
" Kape aff that grass, now, or I 'll run yez in."

A COMPOUND FRACTURE.

RONDEL.

SINCE Amaryllis Smith no more is Smith,
    And wed and fled is sweet Neæra Jones,
I loudly cry that Cupid is a myth,
But secretly I weep his chubby bones
And covertly I make these many moans,
    For of the world I seem not part nor lith
    Since Amaryllis Smith no more is Smith,
And wed and fled is sweet Neæra Jones.
The pumpkin-pie has lost a certain pith ;
    The tender turkey sings in saddened tones ;
The buckwheat batter blooms and bears ; but
      with
    That dearth of flavor all existence owns,
Since Amaryllis Smith no more is Smith,
    And wed and fled is sweet Neæra Jones.

THE TEACHER DID.

A RONDEAU OF A WESTERN SCHOOL.

"HOLD up your hands," the teacher cried,
    And *would* have added this beside,
"You who have been to school at all,"
For young and old and large and small
Had gathered there from near and wide.

It was not easy to divide
The motley throng, so to decide,
He raised his voice in sudden call,
    " Hold up your hands!"

Some children screamed, while others tried
Beneath the furniture to hide;
But one game infant, near the wall,
Pulled forth a " gun " and yelled " By gol!
I haint no tender-footed snide;
    Hold up *your* hands!"

RONDEAU—EN PASSANT.

I KNOW she 'll look. I know it, though
   One well might think she does not know
Whose eyes are on her comeliness
As on she comes, but I can guess
What gives her face that sudden glow.

She 's by. Now will she turn?—Yes—no—
Aha! I smile in glee, for lo!
Her longing she can not repress
         I know she 'll look.

Think not that I 'm a flirt or beau,
Or ogling, cheap Lothario,
Or she—she 's modest to excess;
But I am poor and had to dress
My last year's bonnet over, so
         I *knew* she 'd look.

UNRESPONSIVE.

SHE waved her graceful hand to me
    And glanced and nodded as I passed.
I 'm of a poor and low degree ;
    She with the proudest set is classed.

And yet she waved her hand to me ;
    Fair hand ! which scores have vainly sought,—
And frowned, yes, flushed perchance, to see
    That I passed on and heeded not.

For that hand some would do or die,
    But I am not as others are ;
She waved her hand.   No heed took I,
    But guided on my cable-car.

THE NAKED TRUTH.

POET, thou 'rt like unto a gas-man, for the fleeter
    Thy product runs through *easy-moving meter*,
The more thou grinnest gayly, till, alas!
Thou findest other simile to gas,
And learnedst iambs and dactyls are but meet
To fetch a poor piaster *for a thousand feet.*

"THE RULING PASSION."

GO to, ye men who seek an ordinary woman's " Yes,"
And pity me, ye gentle gods ! *I* loved an editress.
With fervor I implored her to accept my heart and hand ;
Her answer came to me by mail, and thus that answer scanned :

> "Not available at present. No lack of merit necessarily implied. Similar articles already on hand. Often forced to reject what others may use."

I kissed the hand that smote me (or rather, kissed the mitten,)
But demanded back the many fervid letters I had written ;
And gently hinted I might be a more deserving man
To know wherein I failed with *her*, and thus her answer ran :

> "Cannot undertake to give personal criticisms. Stamps must be enclosed to insure return of MSS."

AN AFTERTHOUGHT.

I.—THE DEED.

"SWEETS to the sweet," I pen
   Upon this candy-box
And send it to the fairest, then,
   Who breathes and walks.

II.—REPENTANCE.

"Sweets to the sweet," I penned.
   My fond heart almost stops.
O, fool! to write her thus and send
   Those lemon drops.

SUB ROSA.

YOU would n't think a man like me
    Would let such foolish passion gather,
But—well, I loved Tom's wife and she,
    I thought she seemed to like it rather.

I almost feel her kisses still ;
    That is—O, well, I had to let her.
You see, she really cared until
    One luckless day, and then—Tom met her.

ETYMOLOGY.

WHEN Hebrew bears on Hebrew children used to sup,
The greeting to a prophet was
                  "Go up!"

And had he lived in Shakespeare's time, I hold it true
The salutation would have been
                  "Go to!"

But now these ancient forms are so improved upon,
Elias would be angered with
                  "Go on!"

A "DASHING" MAIDEN.

I 'M a maid of happy summers, not too many, not too few,
I always do the things which people say one ought to do ;
I move in best society, observing all its law,
It really puzzles me to see wherein I have a flaw ;
But someway, somehow, somewhere, Fortune's favor seems to miss me,
  For though I 'm not unsightly,
  Men all treat me *so* politely,
And never one is rude enough to ——

I 'm amicable to foibles, do not deprecate cigars,
Vote a chaperon a nuisance for a walk beneath the stars ;
I can talk with wit or wisdom, not a subject do I shirk,
From the much-enduring weather, up to Browning and his work.
I am maidenly and modest, but, I hope not *too* straight-laced,
  And I own I never thought
  Men were such a prudent lot
That the coat-sleeve never wrapped around ——

Mama tells me I 'm a belle, and brother says I 'm "not so bad,"
And Papa always pays the bills, no matter what the fad ;
I 'm danced and driven, flirted with, no doubt I 'm very gay,
But everything is done in such a *proper* sort of way,
That, though I 'm very happy and would covet nothing rash,
  Still I hope it isn't harmful
  Just to want to be an —
And to feel the tittillation of a bold ——

MY OWN SWEET HEART.

DEAR heart! aye, dearest of the earth!
   Long, long ago I learned thy worth,
And prized it ere my lips could frame
Thy praise—and still I love the same.

None other sends my tingling blood
Its happy course, with joyous flood.
None other yields such sympathy
And pains with all that troubles me.

In days of misery gone by,
By other hearts betrayed was I;
But thou, dear one, will constant be
Till life hath ceased in thee and me.

Yea, I can swear thou 'rt " all my own,"
   And " ever constant to this breast; "
Forsooth, thou beat'st " for me alone "
   Some inches underneath my vest!

THE SADDEST THING.

SADDER than misery Nero heard,
　　Sadder than plaint of an orphaned bird,
Sadder than Day when the Sun's fair face
Disdains her, sadder than Sorrow's trace
On the lips of Love, sadder than Sin,
Sadder than Memory's " might have been,"
Sadder than dark of Error's night,
Sadder than wrong defeating right,
Sadder than Dian's dreamy light,
Sadder than fire and storm and blight,
Sadder than birth to a world of care,
Sadder than death to—oh! who knows where?
Sadder than else which the world contains
Is the joke a man makes—and then explains!

REQUIESCAT IN PACE.

THE man who fears to go his way alone,
    But follows where the greater number tread,
Should hasten to his rest beneath a stone;
    The great majority of men are dead.

"FOUND WANTING."

JEANNE D'ARC lacked an education ;
   Pompadour lacked depth of mind ;
Maintenon lacked toleration ;
   Esther might have been more kind.

Hebrew Sarah lacked humaneness ;
   Good Octavia wanted wit ;
Greek Xantippe lacked urbaneness ;
   Eliot was n't *chic* a bit.

Cleopatra lacked humility ;
   Ruth was minus worldly wealth ;
Bess of England lacked civility ;
   Saint Theresa lacked in health.

Aspasia lacked in social station ;
   Paula lacked in style and fashion ;
De Staël lacked domestication ;
   Phryne *did n't* lack in passion ;—

Polly 's perfect, but, you see
   Lacks *in toto* love for me.

*Some hardy, homely buds find pretty mention,
While perfect blossoms die without attention.*

To MORRIS R. HUGHES, OF CLEVELAND, OHIO,
A MODEL MAN OF BUSINESS, A WISE COUNSELLOR, AND AN EVER GENIAL FRIEND, AND TO MY OTHER FORMER OFFICE-ASSOCIATES, ALMOST BROTHERS, I CORDIALLY DEDICATE THE VERSES FOLLOWING.

THE TENDER-HEARTED MAN.

A PLAIN, rough room ; a plain, smooth box ; aye, both as plain
As he, the dead, who lay as all have lain,
Or will lie, sometime, somewhere.

                              Everything was still
Save where the clock grieved on, as if its will
Would serve no master, since the old one passed
From out that narrow lodgment to his last.

We knew but little of him, for his ways were shy,
But this we knew, that Sundays he passed by
The small, rude church we backwoods folk had made,
And neighbors whispered that he never prayed ;
And so we cast commiserating glances
And whispered fears about his future chances.

But after a while our good old parson rose,
Unschooled, uncultured, but a king to those
Whose only merits have been taught and bred,
And, gazing on the white, worn face, he gently said :

"I don't know what our friend believed. He never made no fuss
Or worry over it, and so it need n't worry us.
He may have been a Baptist, or have taken Calvin's creed,
Or maybe him and Ingersoll, as like as not, agreed.
He may have thought God made us, or we simply just began;
But, right or wrong, he allus was a tender-hearted man.

"When he saw a cripple comin', did he walk fast and straight,
As a half unconscious slight upon the other fellow's gait?
No, sir! He'd sort of lag along by that poor chap and smile,
Like he liked to beat the record for the slowest-goin' mile.
It was n't much, but that's just it. It's doin' what you can
That goes to make the value of a tender-hearted man.

"When a beggar-man 'ud ask him, he did n't smell 'nd shrink
And say he'd give a nickel, if it did n't go for drink.
When he saw a fallen mortal he did n't quote a text;
He helped him up, and said, 'Who knows but I may be the next?

Who knows how long this brother fought, or how his fault began?
Who knows that *he* could conquer?' said this tender-hearted man.

"A half-growed, half-starved kitten and the sparrow it had caught
'Ud both stir up the bottom of his feelin' and his thought.
'Such awful things is in the world,' he'd say, and almost cry;
'It's mighty hard that little cat or else the bird must die.
This world beats me, but anyhow, though we don't know its plan,
Let's stop a little trouble,' says this tender-hearted man.

"He made mistakes and had his sins, but never claimed to be
The one man in the universe that had the right idee;
He never aimed at greatness and you wouldn't call him smart,
But if he lacked a hundred ways, he made it up in heart,
For you can search your little world, from Beersheba to Dan,
And can't find none too many of the tender-hearted man."

And though no word our parson spoke had given
A promise that this soul had found a Heaven,
No hope of golden gates, or music of the blest,
Or ways of asphodel of happy rest,
We felt, whatever lay beyond our sight,
The tender-hearted man had gone aright.

OVER THE GET-THERE ROAD.

WHO will dare the road to There,
    The There of glittering glory?
Rough it is as a Whitman ode,
Cruel it is as the Russian code,
Long it is as the devil's goad;
At least, so runs the story.
There's never a finger-post nor guide,
Nor beast to bear your load;
Beware of the Reckless Rapid's tide
And of Easy Swamp on the other side;
Go slow and sure, for you cannot ride
    Over the Get-There Road.

What's the fare to get to There,
The There of marvellous mention?
Only a soul of smallest breed,
Only a life of grasping greed,
Only a heart which does not heed
Another's right or plight or need,
But holds its own intention.

I saw one left to a loathsome pest,
For that is Get-There mode.
One picked the purse of his wretched guest,
One trod rough-shod on a sweetheart's breast,
    Over the Get-There Road.

What's the share of those of There?
Why, every taste is suited;
Flaming fame or a ruling rod,
A sunny smile of the golden god,
Or may be six by two of sod,
For that's a point disputed.
There's never a way to tell what's true
Of that select abode,
Till you pass the wall which bars its view,
Over or under, around or through.
I don't know how it is done, do you?
Most of us don't, but some of us do,
    Over the Get-There Road.

Then who would care to get to There?
Why, *all*, if truth be spoken.
Spite of scornful gibe and sneer
There must have a heartsome cheer,
And can't be worse than being here
By many a sign and token.
Then ho! for a tramp on a well-worn track,

Though rough as a Whitman ode,
Or cruel as the Russian code,
Or long as the devil's goad,
Whatever it is, there 's nothing back,
It can't be worse than a *cul de sac*,
So, gird up your loins, pick up your pack,
    And hey for the Get-There Road!

THE ASCETIC—UP TO DATE.

O, what is the guard for a soul pressed hard,
    When the devil comes a-wooing?
And why do I lack to buffet him back,
    When I know what the fiend is doing?

In the shaded gloom of my narrow room,
    I sit for aye and ever ;
Yea, yea, for I swore that past its door
    I would wander never—never.

Yet I sometimes look from the tiring book
    Beyond the half-swung casement ;
And mine eye and ear, and the devil near,
    All tempt to my soul's abasement.

Ah, yes! It is clear that eye and ear
    Are leagued with the cunning devil,
And the modest gloom of my well-kept room
    They would turn to a carnal revel.

THE ASCETIC—UP TO DATE.

O, why should the mind be so inclined
   To what it forswore forever?
And why should the flesh be a constant mesh
   To tangle the soul's endeavor?

When up to my cell comes a fragrant smell
   Of the weed which is ever burning,
O, why does it serve to set each nerve
   On edge with a hungry yearning?

O, why does the shine in the depths of wine,
   Of which I am set to thinking,
Turn all my blood to a fiery flood,
   When I do not approve of drinking?

For, indeed, I know 't is the seed of woe,
   From the simplest sin to slaughter;
And yet I am cursed with a deep, deep thirst,
   Which is n't appeased by water.

O, why does the flirt of a muslin skirt,
   And the glimpse of a tapered ankle,
Send a sudden zest to disturb the breast,
   And to lie in the heart and rankle?

O, why do I sigh when the world goes by
   With all of its feathers flying,
When I know it sold its soul for gold
   On the scales of theft and lying?

And why is it now that I still allow
 The whisper that tempts abasement :
" You only swore not to pass the door,
 But still there is left—the casement !"

. . . .

Ah, devil, you lie, for *the room is I*,
 And though I must listen to you,
The living thrill of determined will
 Shall soon or late undo you.

And that is the guard for a soul pressed hard
 When the devil, Self, comes wooing,
For who can fly the restraint of " I,"
 Except to his own undoing ?

THE OTHER ONE WAS BOOTH.

NOW, by the rood, as Hamlet says, it grieves me sore to say
The stage is not as once it was when *I* was wont to play.
'T is true that Irving, dear old chap, still gives a decent show,
And Mansfield and young Willard really act the best they know;
'T is true, Dusé and Bernhardt, for we must n't be too hard,
Are very fair, for women, though of course they ought to guard
Against some bad-art tendencies; and as for all the rest,
There's hardly one, I may say none, who stands the artist's test.
True artists are a rare, rare breed; there were but two, forsooth,
In all *my* time, the stage's prime! and the other one was Booth.

Why, Mac—I mean Macready—but we always called him Mac;
And old Ned Forrest used to say, or so they once told Jack;

Or, that is, Jack McCullough—well, this is what they said:
There were but two who really knew how Shakespeare should be read.
They did n't mean the younger Kean nor Jack; and so perhaps
It caused a little jealousy among the lesser chaps.
They said that Lawrence Barrett was entitled to respect;
But as for Tom Salvini, well, his dago dialect
Would never do for Shakespeare; so, to tell the simple truth,
There were only two men in it; and the other one was Booth.

Don't think conceit is in me tongue. 'T is something I detest;
But I may say that in me day I 've figured with the best.
Why, Kalamazoo, and Oshkosh, too, and Kankakee as well,
Went fairly wild, nor man nor child stirred when the curtain fell.
The S. R. O. was hung each night; our show was such a rage
They took the ushers off the floor and ushered from the stage!

From Kissimee to San Louee, from Nawrleans to Duluth,
Just two stars hit a little bit; and the other one was Booth.

I liked Ed Booth, for he was such a royal-hearted fellow,
We never had a jealousy. When he put on Othello.
His Iago was much like to mine, likewise his stage direction;
But what cared Ed what critics said, since *I* made no objection!
Ah, me! That day is past; the play has lost its honored station:
Who reads aright, rage, sorrow, fright, or tragic desolation?
Aye, who can reach to Hamlet's speech, " To be or not to be?"
Or wild Macbeth's cry, "Never shake thy gory locks at me!"
Or Lear's appeal: "Oh, let me not be mad, sweet heavens, not mad!"
Or Shylock's rage: "I'll have me bond!" Ah, me! it makes me sad
To think it all, and then recall the drama of me youth,
When there were *two* who read lines true; and the other one was Booth.

A COURTIN' CALL.

HIM!

HE dressed hisself from top ter toe
 To beat the lates' fash'n.
He give his boots a extry glow,
His dicky glistered like the snow,
He slicked his hair exactly *so*,
 An' all ter indicate "his pash'n."
He tried his hull three ties afore
He kep' the one on that he wore.

HER!

All afternoon she laid abed
 To make her featturs brighter.
She tried on ev'ry geoun she hed,
She rasped her nails until she bled,
A dozen times she frizzed her head

An' put on stuff to make her whiter,
An' fussed till she 'd 'a' cried, she said,
But that 'ld make her eyes so red.

. . . . . .

THEM!

They sot together in the dark
'Ithout a light, excep' their spark,
An' neither could have told er guessed
What way the t'other un was dressed!

THE OLD MAN KNOWS.

DAN, yu 'll never find another
    Like the hand of good old mother,
Which hez labored fer yer bread,
Yes, more 'n that, 'f all b' said,
Fer she won 'nd then she made it;
'Nd such bread! yu would n't trade it
Fer no bankwit, if yu knew
How yu 'll ache for 't when she 's through
Doin' fer yu. Don't yu s'pose
Like enough the old man knows?

Yes, I know it ain't ez milky
In its looks, ner yet ez silky
In its feel, ez 't use' to be,
But 'f these old eyes can see
Ev'ry line 's a line of beauty,
Er a mark fer well done duty.
No use talkin', Dan, it 's so.
Guess the old man ought to know.

THE OLD MAN KNOWS.

'Nd how ev'ry faded finger
Loves to touch yu 'nd to linger
In yer hair. Yu 'll understand
Better some day 'bout that hand.
Nothin' else can do ez much ez
Them same peacefil, tender touches.
How they soothe 'nd how old Sorro'
Sneaks until some sad to-morro'.
Dan, O Dan, the old man knows;
He hed a mother, don't yu s'pose?

LAUGH A LITTLE BIT.

HERE 'S a motto, just your fit—
  Laugh a little bit.
When you think you 're trouble hit,
Laugh a little bit.
Look misfortune in the face.
Brave the beldam's rude grimace ;
Ten to one 't will yield its place,
If you have the wit and grit
Just to laugh a little bit.

Keep your face with sunshine lit,
Laugh a little bit.
All the shadows off will flit,
If you have the grit and wit
Just to laugh a little bit.

Cherish this as sacred writ—
Laugh a little bit.
Keep it with you, sample it,
Laugh a little bit.
Little ills will sure betide you,
Fortune may not sit beside you,
Men may mock and fame deride you,
But you 'll mind them not a whit
If you laugh a little bit.

*And here's a bunch of posies of and for the youngest of us.
Long may they crow it over us and worry us and love us.*

To Herbert Wilbur Porter,

"OUR BABY,"

AND TO ALL HIS FELLOWS WHO ARE GROWING UP TO-DAY TO MAKE THE WORLD GREATER AND BETTER TO-MORROW.

LEOPOLD.

THIS is the story of Leopold,
    A man of the world, just five years old,
A little bit wise and a little bit bold,
Who wanted a guinea of gold.

Poor little, sad little five-year-old,
Of woes of avarice never told,
Too much charmed by gleamy gold,
Wanted one piece to have and to hold.

Papa might laugh, and mamma might scold,
Toys grow tarnished or gray with mold,
Porridge be hot or porridge be cold,
Little cared little Leopold.

Out of the house the boykin strolled,
And round and round the blue eyes rolled,
Always looking for gold, gold, gold.

Money was everywhere—wealth untold—
Copper and silver, and glistening gold,
Greedily grasped and stingily doled,
Cheated for, fought for, bought and sold.

Across the counters it slid and rolled;
And big iron safes looked cross and cold
And stretched their arms to catch and hold,
As a miser does, the gleamy gold.
And who could have forced or who cajoled
One piece from their grasping, clasping hold?

Tired, so tired, grew our five-year-old;
Hunting feet should be harder soled;
And the big church bell the death-knell tolled
Of by-gone hours, till at last he strolled
Into a street of another mold
Where nothing was bought and nothing sold.

"Ho!" sniffed sad little Leopold,
As if to say that to search for gold
In a place where none of it round him rolled
Were foolish in a wise five-year-old.

He turned to go, when lo, and behold!
Down at his feet in the untrod mold
Lay a bright guinea of gold! gold! gold!

But no one ever has seen or told
Of a happy hunter after gold ;
" I want some more ! " cried Leopold.

Now are n't we all like five-year-old,
After something gleamy as gold ?
And perhaps the prize we hope to hold
Is down the street we have n't strolled ;
So be a bit wise and a little bit bold,
But *don't* be greedy like Leopold !

THE NEW ST. NICHOLAS.

'TWAS Christmas Eve and Nicholas Claus
    Went back to his store from the boarding-house.

Trade was poor and Christmas cheer
Was not for a man with a losing year.
Lessening cash and growing debt
Never made any man happy yet.
Growing expense and lessening sales ;
He scowled his brow and bit his nails.
Creditors pressing and debtors slow ;
He slammed his desk and he turned to go,
And said, addressing the nearest wall,
" What 's the use of trying at all ?

I wish this weary life were past ;
I wish this Christmas were my last."
When, drifting in on a wintry blast
Came the fairest mite of a fairy girl.
Golden hair in a tangled curl ;

Shoes unbuttoned, but face as bright
As the fairest star on the clearest night.

"Well?" said Nicholas, after a pause.
"Pease, sir, is oo dood Mister Tlaws?"
"'Claws,' they call me, little mouse,
Who don't know the honest Dutch of 'Klowse,'
But how in the mischief came you here
And how do you know my name, my dear?"

The little maid answered, "Knows it, tause
Me knows how to spell it, Mister Tlaws.
Mama teached me; she knows, I dess,
Zere's a c, an' a l, an' a a-oo-s,
An' I seened it on oor window-pane.
An' pease, Mister Tlaws, won't oo etsplain
How ve 'ittle deers an' sled tan fly?
An' tan vey ever fly up so high
As mama an' me is, way up top
Free floors over ve drocery shop?"

"People and deer can do great things
If only they try—though they don't have wings,
And what would you want the deer to take
You and your mama? Apples and cake,
A doll and a hobby-horse, candy, too?
How do you think that list would do?"

The little one's eyes grew wide and bright
At bare suggestion of such delight,
But she closed her lips and shook her head.
"*Me yants a sown-achine*," she said.
"A big man bringed us yun, yun day,
But n'uzzer man taked it all away.
An' w'en he was don', my mama c'yed,
An' me tlimbed up, an' ast her why 'd
She c'y, and *she* says 'Tause wese poor.'
So pease, Mister Tlaws, won't oo brin' yun to 'er?"

Nicholas swallowed hard and felt
His eyes grow warm and moist and melt
Over his lashes. Down he bent
And picking the little tot up, he went
Out to the stable, saying, "Here
Is Queenie. She'll do instead of deer."

Into the harness went the mare
And into the sleigh our worthy pair,
With the best machine in the goodly house
Of his new found saintship,—Nicholas Claus.
"Now tuck in good from this driving snow
And tell me which is the way to go."

"Ooh!" said the child with an injured look,
"Is n't us down in oor 'ittle book?"

"Bless my soul, but I quite forgot
To look the address up, little tot.
You'll have to show me." So she showed
The way to carry the precious load,
And Nicholas tip-toed three flights high
And set it down; then breathed, "Good-bye,
Little heroine-baby; better go in
Or mama won't know where on earth you 've been."

Her little head took a bashful tip,
And a finger sought the rosebud lip;
Then shyly patting one of his knees,
The little maid said, "Tan't me tiss oo, pease?"

Nicholas clasped her close and tight,
And the darling laughed her pure delight,
And said, "Tan't me tall oo 'Santy,' 'tause
Me lites oo *so* much, Mister Tlaws."

A happier man than Nicholas Claus
Never went home to a boarding-house.
But first he arranged for a Christmas pack
To be sent to the girl on the fourth floor back;
And he stabled Queenie, and fixed her right
To stand the rigorous winter night,
And bought a dozen newsboys out,
Greeted his friends with a cheery shout,

And laughed and said, " By George, it's queer
That the biggest credit I've got this year
Is charged to Profit and Loss account;
For the entry of that one small amount
Has balanced all of my woes. I'll start
All over again, with a braver heart.

So, dear little girl, thy gift to me
Is far, far more than mine to thee."

A WATCHWORD.

When you find a certain lack
    In the stiffness of your back
At a threatened fierce attack,
Just the hour
That you need your every power,
Look a bit
For a thought to baffle it.
Just recall that every knave,
Every coward, can be brave,
Till the time
That his courage should be prime—
Then 't is fled.
Keep your head!
What a folly 't is to lose it
Just the time you want to use it!

When the ghost of some old shirk
Comes to plague you, and to lurk
In your study or your work,
Here 's a hit
Like enough will settle it.

Knowledge is a worthy prize ;
Knowledge comes to him who tries—
Whose endeavor
Ceases never.
Everybody would be wise
As his neighbor,
Were it not that they who labor
For the trophy creep, creep, creep,
While the others lag or sleep ;
And the sun comes up some day
To behold one on his way
Past the goal
Which the soul
Of another has desired,
But whose motto was, " I 'm tired."

When the task of keeping guard
Of your heart—
Keeping weary watch and ward
Of the part
You are called upon to play
Every day—
Is becoming dry and hard,
Conscience languid, virtue irksome,
Good behaviour growing *worksome*,—
Think this thought :
Doubtless everybody could,

A WATCHWORD.

Doubtless everybody would,
Be superlatively good,
Were it not
That it's harder keeping straight
Than it is to deviate;
And to keep the way of right,
You must have the pluck to *fight*.

CONSOLATION.

ONE day in December
    (I don't just remember
The date), and somewhere near the top of the map,
    Good Santa was sitting
    Preparing for flitting,
And he pasted his calling-list snug in his cap.

    The saint was a sightly
    Old fellow, and brightly
His nimbus shone out from his jolly old poll,
    But having done conning
    His list, again donning
His cap, lo! his halo was *doused*, and the scroll
    Was burned rather badly
    And *two* names so sadly
That the saint could n't puzzle 'em out, for his soul.

    I 'd not be a breeder
    Of pardons, my reader,
For even a saint, when his duty is missed,
    But should Santy neglect
    To bring what we expect,
Perhaps your name and mine were those lost from the list.

"ON THE JUDGMUNT DAY."

"THAT Jim Young 's a mean old thing.
    What you think he done?
He knocked my alley out the ring
'N' grabbed it up 'n' run.
An' it was n't keepses, like he says it was;
Keeps is wicked gamblin'; knows it, too, he does.
Why 'd he run away for, if he thought tuz fair?
He 's a *mean, old* cheater, now! but I don't care.
He 'll git ketched up sometime where he can't run 'way;
He 'll *git a lickin'* on the Judgmunt Day.

"What you laughin' at? It 's so.
If you 're bad er naughty!
Guess my mother ought to know,
'N' she tol' me 'n' Tottie
Not to tell no stories, ner to say bad things,
Ner hook the groc'ry apples, ner to pull flies' wings,
Ner b'unpolite to comp'ny, ner walk the railroad ties,
Ner to fight—spechly fellers not yer size—
Ner never go a swimmin', 'less she says we may,
Er *we 'd* git a lickin' on the Judgmunt Day.

"Joey Smith, he's orful bad.
He's mucher badder 'n me.
He's a stealer. Oncet he had
Two birdnests from our tree,
An' the little 'cheepses'—course they could n't fly—
Jus' was lef' there, nakid, on the groun' to die.
I was *jus' as mad* as ever I could be.
I'd a *killed* that feller! but he's bigger 'n me.
I don't care. He'll catch it. 'N' so 'll Grace 'n' Nell,
'Cause they tol' I whispered, 'n' they *oughtent* tell.
'N' I was kep' at recess, so 's I could n't play;
Teacher 'll git a lickin' on the Judgmunt Day.

"If I'm good as sugar, say!
Wun't I have the fun
Watchin' other chaps that day
When the lickin 's done?
Gee! I'll do 't. I'll try to allus 'use the mat,'
Keep the ten commandments, never plague the cat,
Take good care of Tottie, not play games too rough—
Be like grannie tells me, 'n' if *that* ain't good 'nough,
I'll jus' walk up, yessir, up to God 'n' say,
'I'm here to take my lickin!' on the Judgmunt Day."

"AUFWIEDERSEH'N."

"AUFWIEDERSEH'N."

KIND word of hope, "Aufwiederseh'n,"
    Reminding we shall meet again.
I would thy constant spell could bless
Each fading, fleeting happiness,
Like loyal, loving lips, which press
And only part to re-caress.

The sun sinks down and all is night,
But lo! in Heaven's awesome height
His splendors in the stars remain
As Nature's grand "Aufwiederseh'n."

So would I have thy presence lend
Its solace, even to the end;
And when one passes, pray detain
The thought of those who still remain
And rob the parting of its pain
With thy sweet hope,
                "Aufwiederseh'n."

www.ingramcontent.com/pod-product-compliance
Lightning Source LLC
Chambersburg PA
CBHW020900160426
43192CB00007B/1013